BUILDING BLOCKS OF COMPUTER SCIENCE

ALGORITHMS

Written by Echo Elise González

Illustrated by Graham Ross

a Scott Fetzer company
Chicago

World Book, Inc.
180 North LaSalle Street
Suite 900
Chicago, Illinois 60601
USA

For information about other World Book publications, visit our website at **www.worldbook.com** or call **1-800-WORLDBK (967-5325)**.
For information about sales to schools and libraries, call 1-800-975-3250 (United States), or 1-800-837-5365 (Canada).

Library of Congress Cataloging-in-Publication Data for this volume has been applied for.

Building Blocks of Computer Science
ISBN: 978-0-7166-2883-5 (set, hc.)

Algorithms
ISBN: 978-0-7166-3382-2

Also available as:
ISBN: 978-0-7166-2893-4 (e-book)

1st printing August 2020

STAFF

Executive Committee
President: Geoff Broderick
Vice President, Finance: Donald D. Keller
Vice President, Marketing: Jean Lin
Vice President, International Sales: Maksim Rutenberg
Vice President, Technology: Jason Dole
Director, Editorial: Tom Evans
Director, Human Resources: Bev Ecker

Editorial
Manager, New Content: Jeff De La Rosa
Writer: Echo Elise González
Proofreader: Nathalie Strassheim

Digital
Director, Digital Product Development: Erika Meller
Digital Product Manager: Jon Wills

Graphics and Design
Sr. Visual Communications Designer: Melanie Bender
Coordinator, Design Development and Production: Brenda B. Tropinski
Sr. Web Designer/Digital Media Developer: Matt Carrington

Acknowledgments:
Art by Graham Ross/The Bright Agency
Series reviewed by Peter Jang/Actualize Coding Bootcamp

TABLE OF CONTENTS

There is a glossary on page 30. Terms defined in the glossary are in type **that looks like this** on their first appearance.

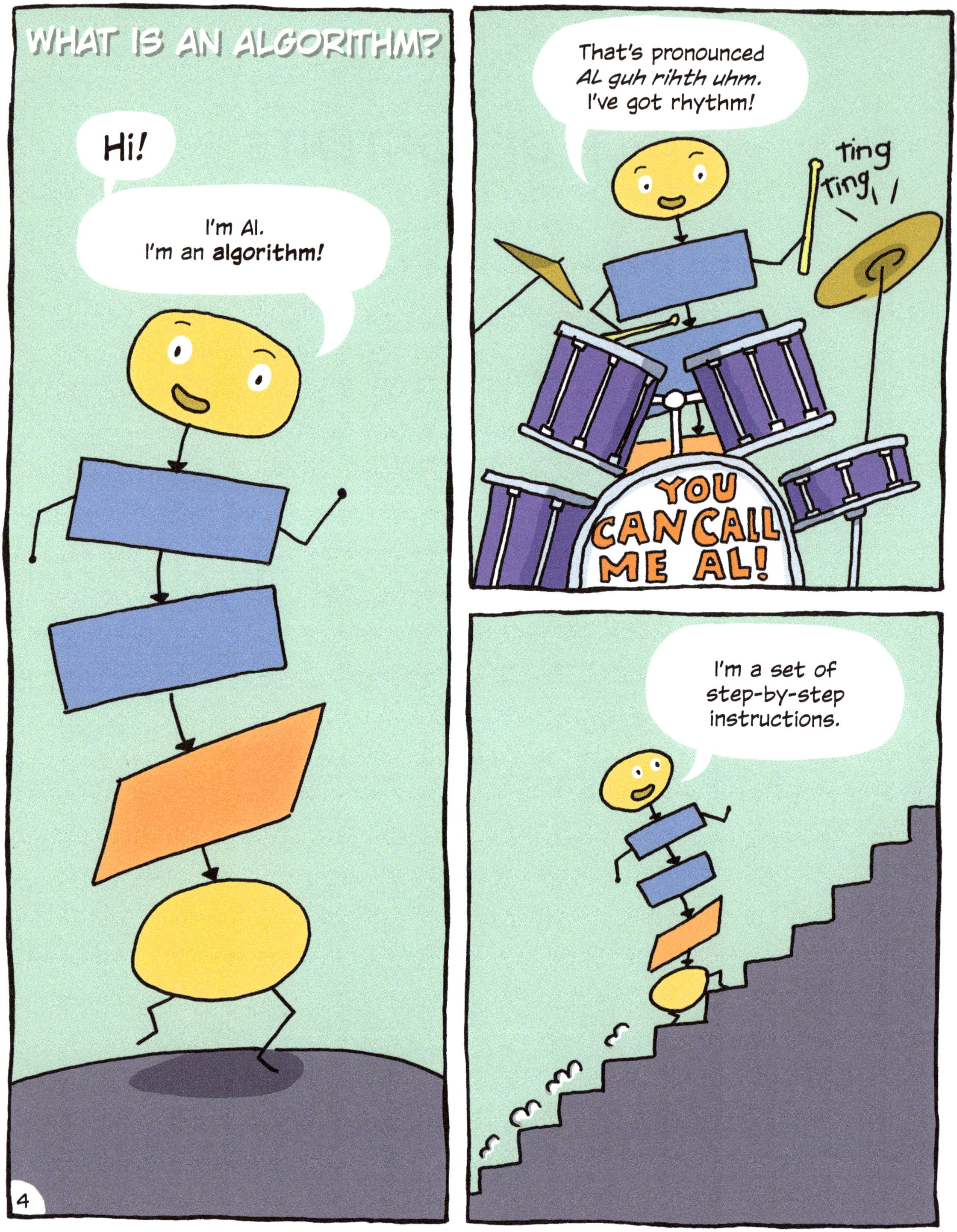

WHAT IS AN ALGORITHM?

Hi!

I'm Al.
I'm an **algorithm!**

I can help solve math problems...
THINKING CAP
8+1/2(12)=x
8+6=x

Or I can tell a computer what to do.

People use me to organize and plan out their actions on the computer and in real life.
The Plan

What can I say? I'm a helpful guy. ...I'm an algorithm!
HELP DESK
AL

To make an algorithm, they have to think like a computer—in simple steps.

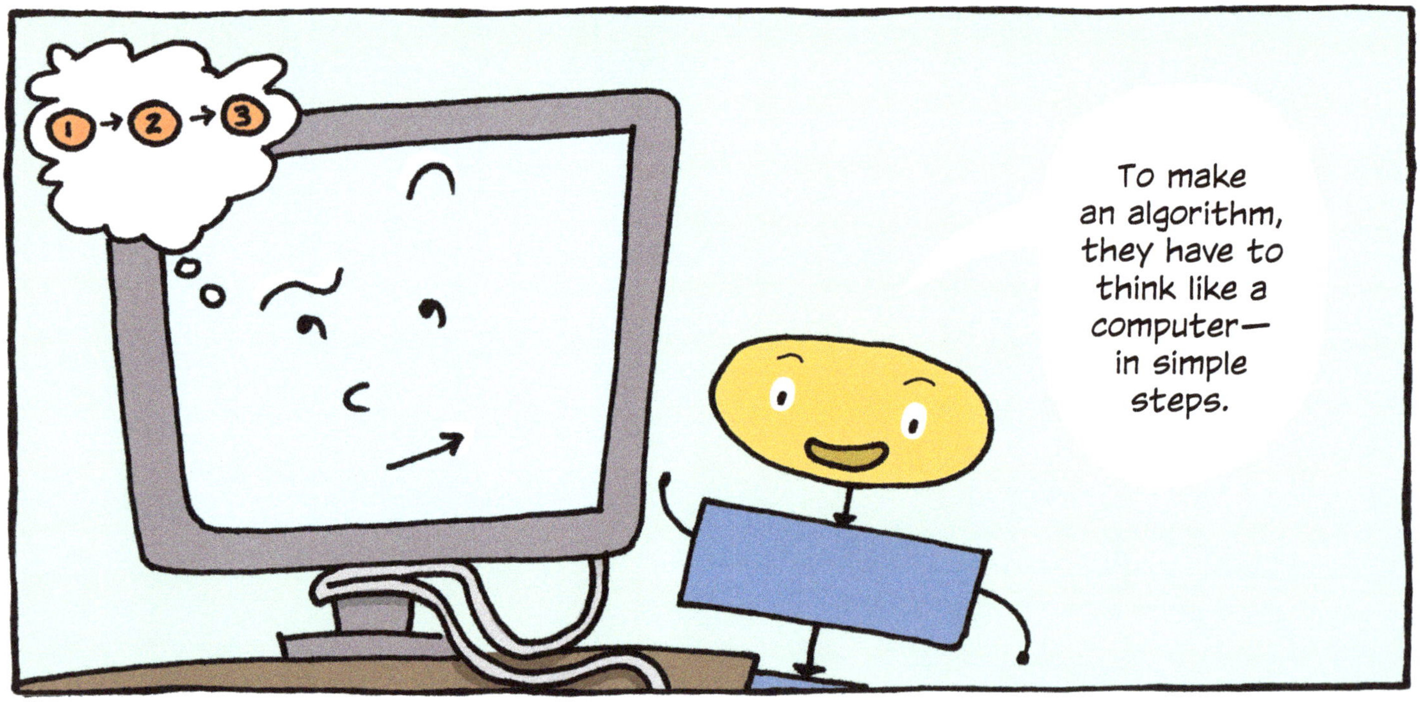

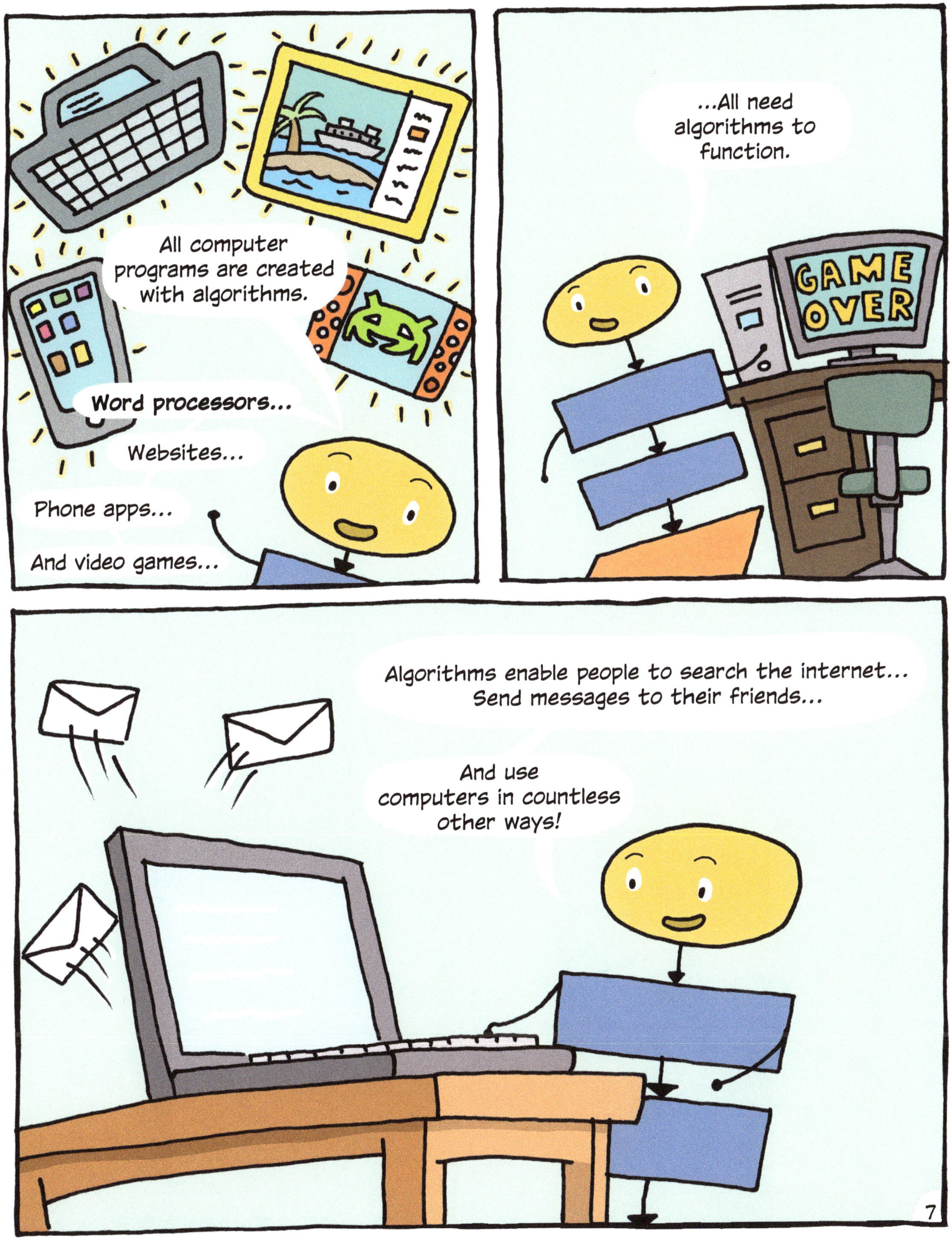

Algorithms enable people to search the internet... Send messages to their friends...

And use computers in countless other ways!

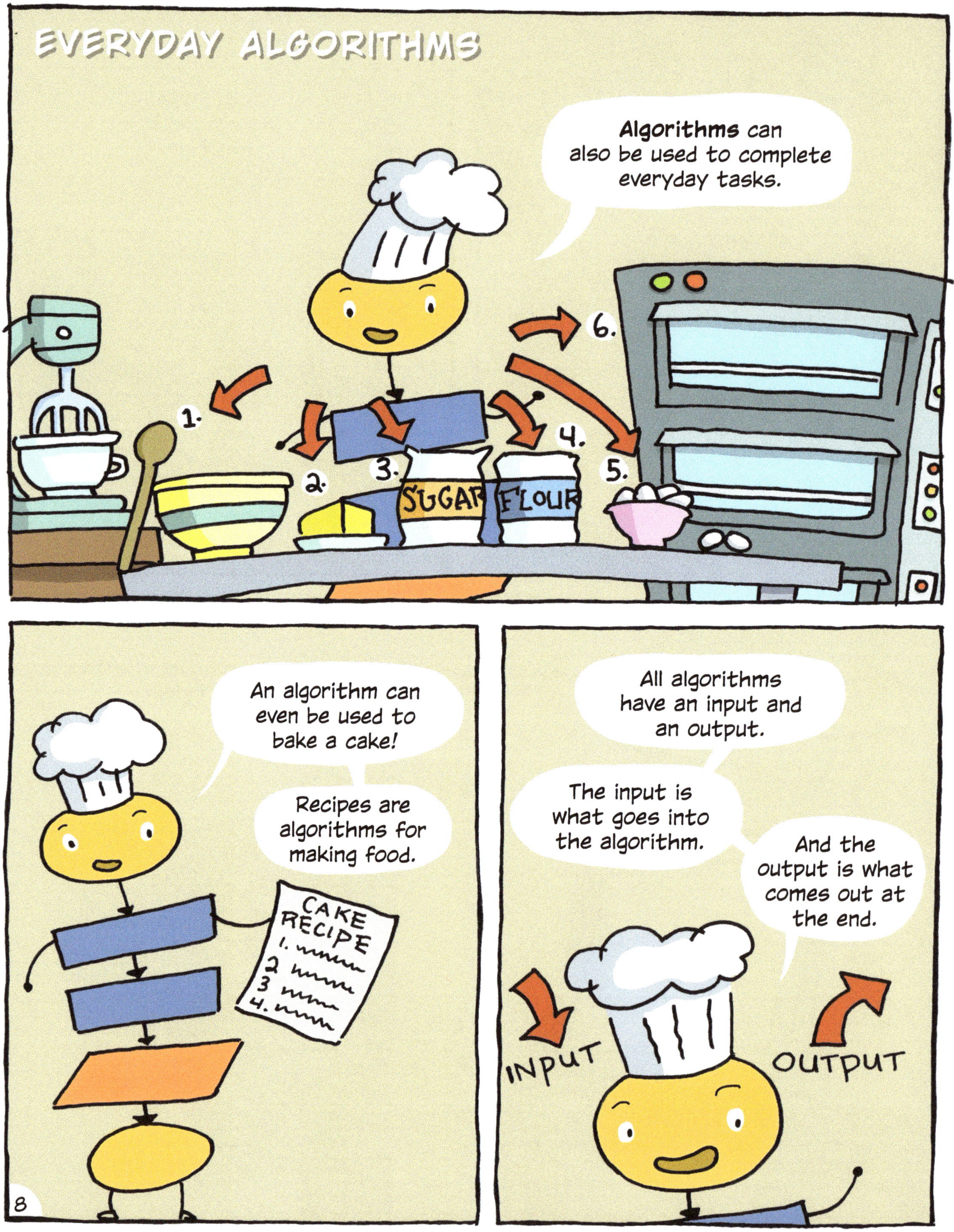

EVERYDAY ALGORITHMS

Algorithms can also be used to complete everyday tasks.

1\.
2\.
3\.
4\.
5\.
6\.
SUGAR
FLOUR

In a cake recipe, the input is the baking tools and the ingredients.
FLOUR
SUGAR
If the algorithm is good...
And the steps are followed correctly...
Recipes
Then the output is...
A CAKE

WRITING ALGORITHMS

Programmers write **algorithms** in **code.**

But algorithms can also be written in different ways.

One way to write an algorithm is by using **pseudocode** (SOO doh code).

In pseudocode, instructions are written out line by line.

Each line describes one step of the algorithm.

Here's an algorithm for playing fetch with a dog, written in pseudocode.

STEP 1: Begin playing fetch.

STEP 2: Throw the ball.

STEP 3: Wait for the dog to return the ball.

STEP 4: Take the ball from the dog.

STEP 5: If you are tired stop playing fetch Otherwise go back to STEP 2.

Pseudocode is written using language that people can understand.

But computers can't understand languages written for people.

DICTIONARY

A computer programmer must translate the pseudocode into a **programming language** so the computer can understand it.

tap tap tap

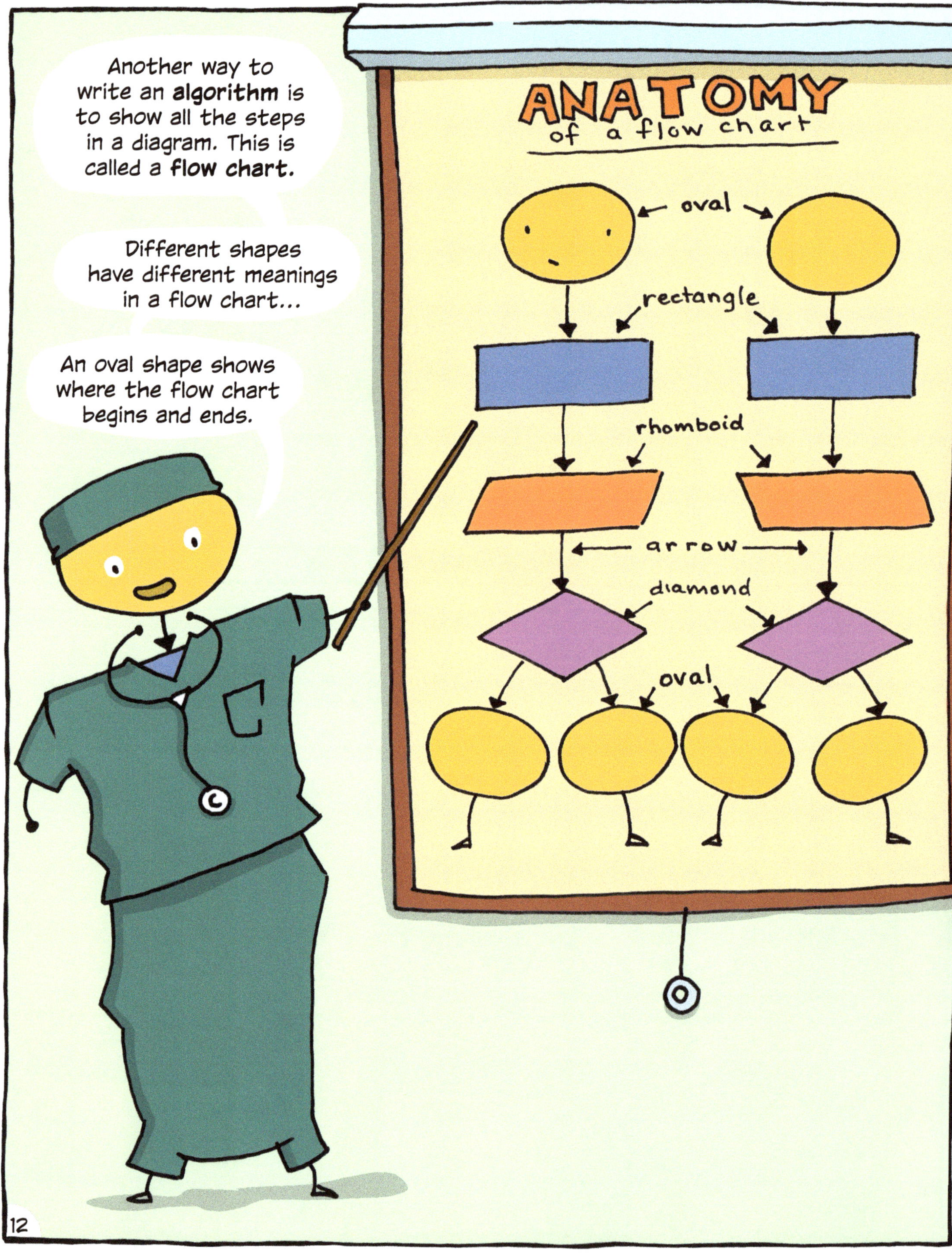
Another way to write an **algorithm** is to show all the steps in a diagram. This is called a **flow chart.**
Different shapes have different meanings in a flow chart...
An oval shape shows where the flow chart begins and ends.
ANATOMY of a flow chart
oval
rectangle
rhomboid
arrow
diamond
oval

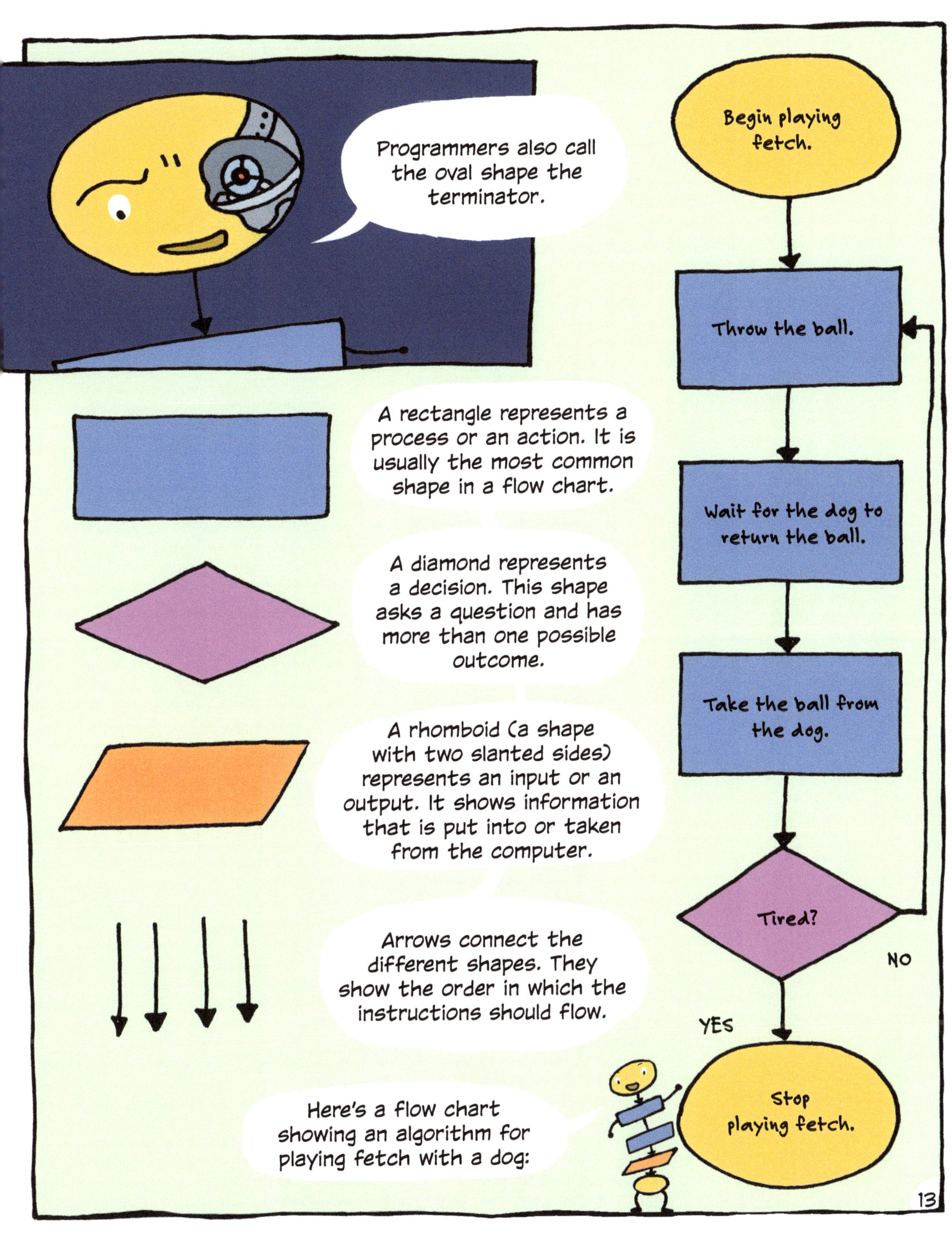

Programmers also call the oval shape the terminator.
A rectangle represents a process or an action. It is usually the most common shape in a flow chart.
A diamond represents a decision. This shape asks a question and has more than one possible outcome.
A rhomboid (a shape with two slanted sides) represents an input or an output. It shows information that is put into or taken from the computer.
Arrows connect the different shapes. They show the order in which the instructions should flow.
Here's a flow chart showing an algorithm for playing fetch with a dog:
Begin playing fetch.
Throw the ball.
Wait for the dog to return the ball.
Take the ball from the dog.
Tired?
NO
YES
Stop playing fetch.

EFFICIENT ALGORITHMS

Each step in an **algorithm** has to be *specific and clear*, so the computer can understand the steps and carry them out correctly.

This is my friend, Tasky the Robot.

BEEP BOOOOOP!

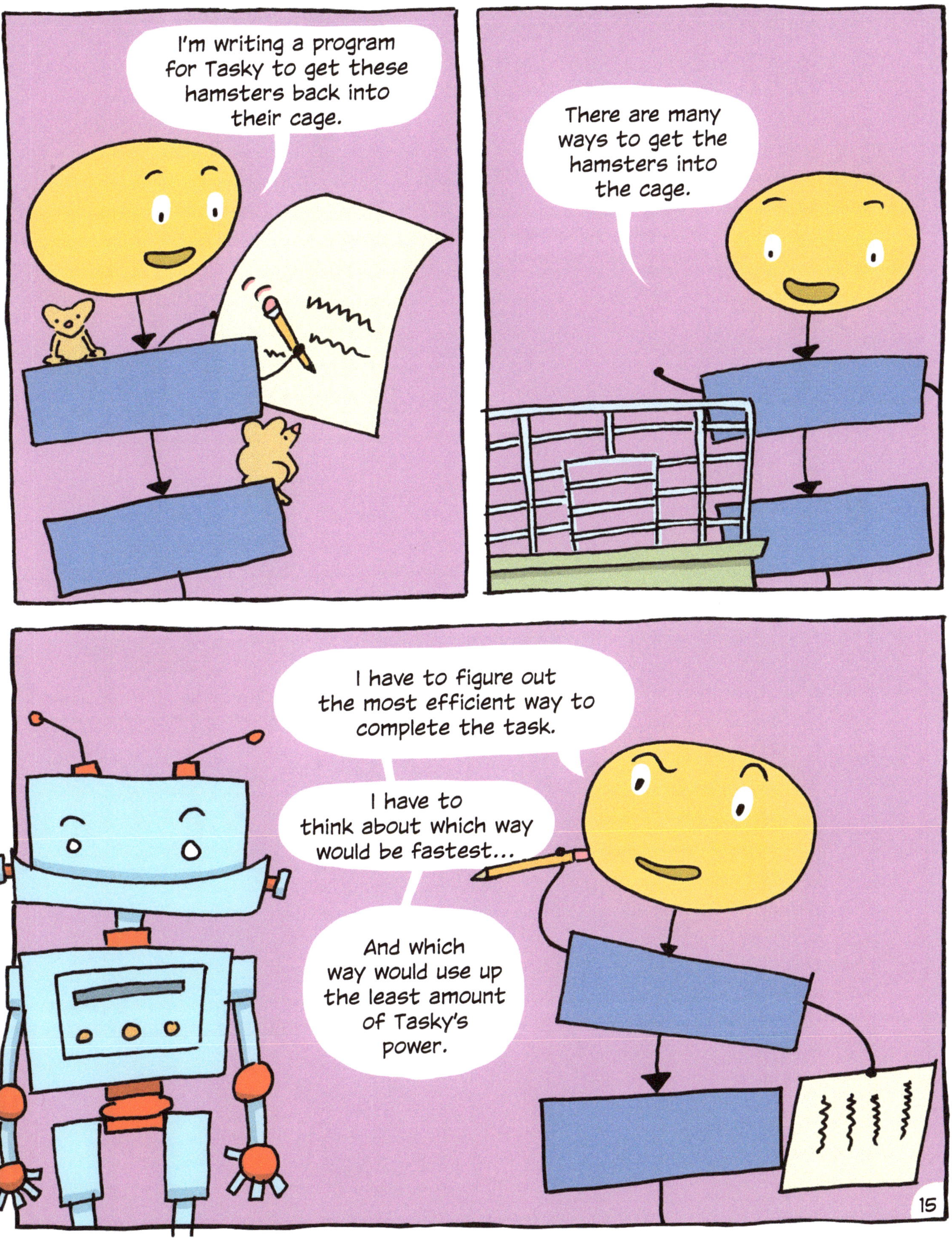

I have to figure out the most efficient way to complete the task.

I have to think about which way would be fastest...

And which way would use up the least amount of Tasky's power.

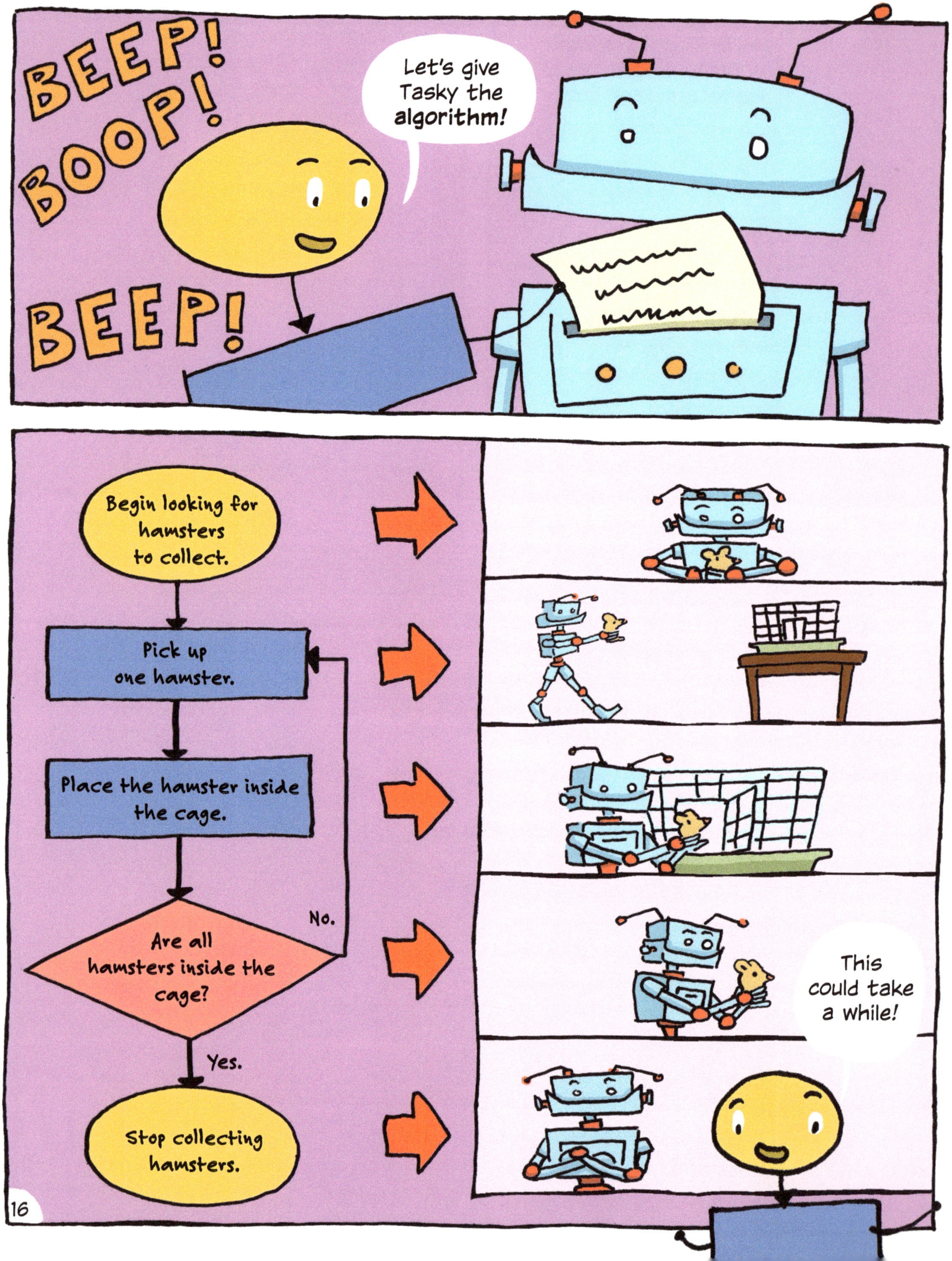

Begin looking for hamsters to collect.

Pick up one hamster.

Place the hamster inside the cage.

Are all hamsters inside the cage?

No.

Yes.

Stop collecting hamsters.

This could take a while!

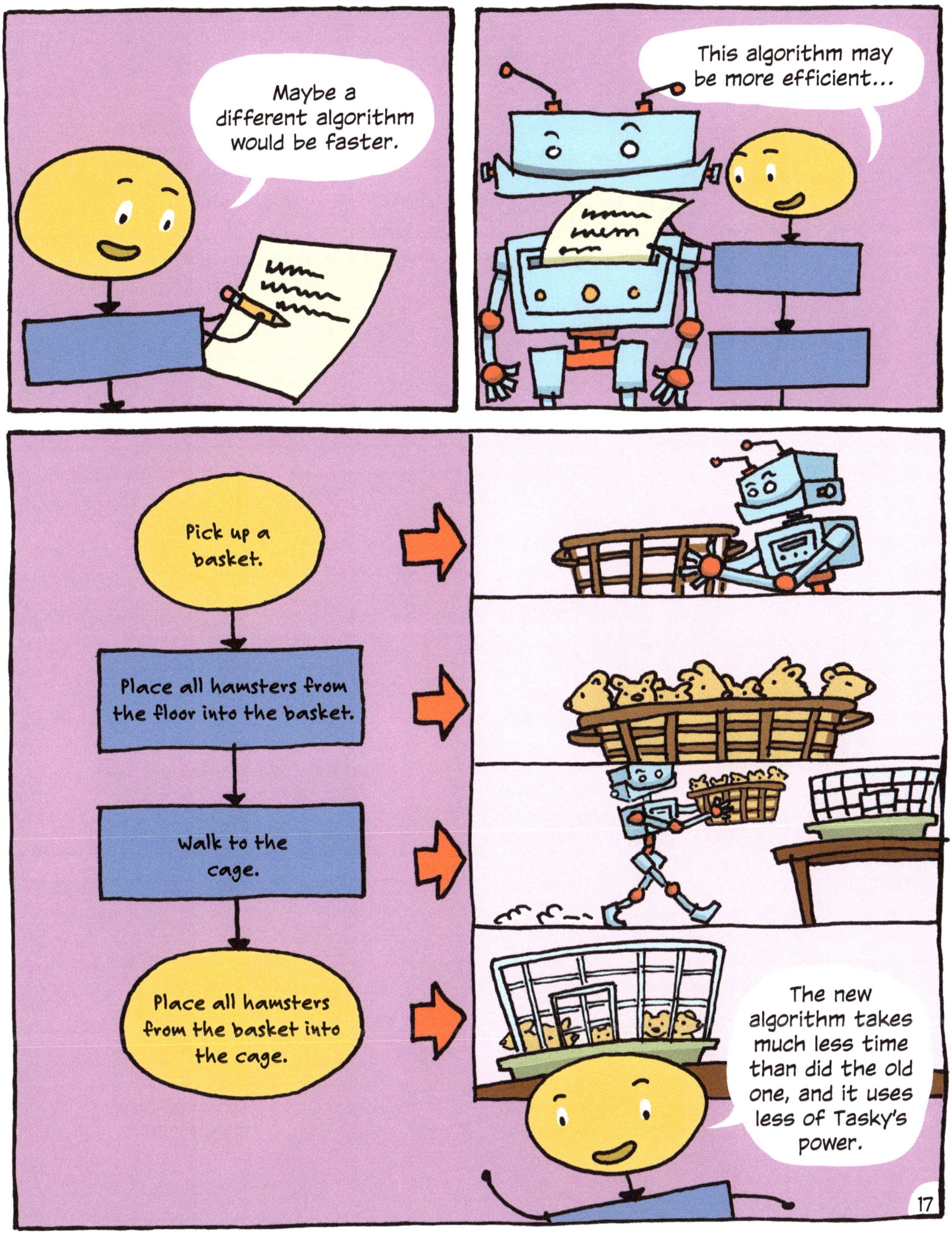

Pick up a basket.

Place all hamsters from the floor into the basket.

Walk to the cage.

Place all hamsters from the basket into the cage.

The new algorithm takes much less time than did the old one, and it uses less of Tasky's power.

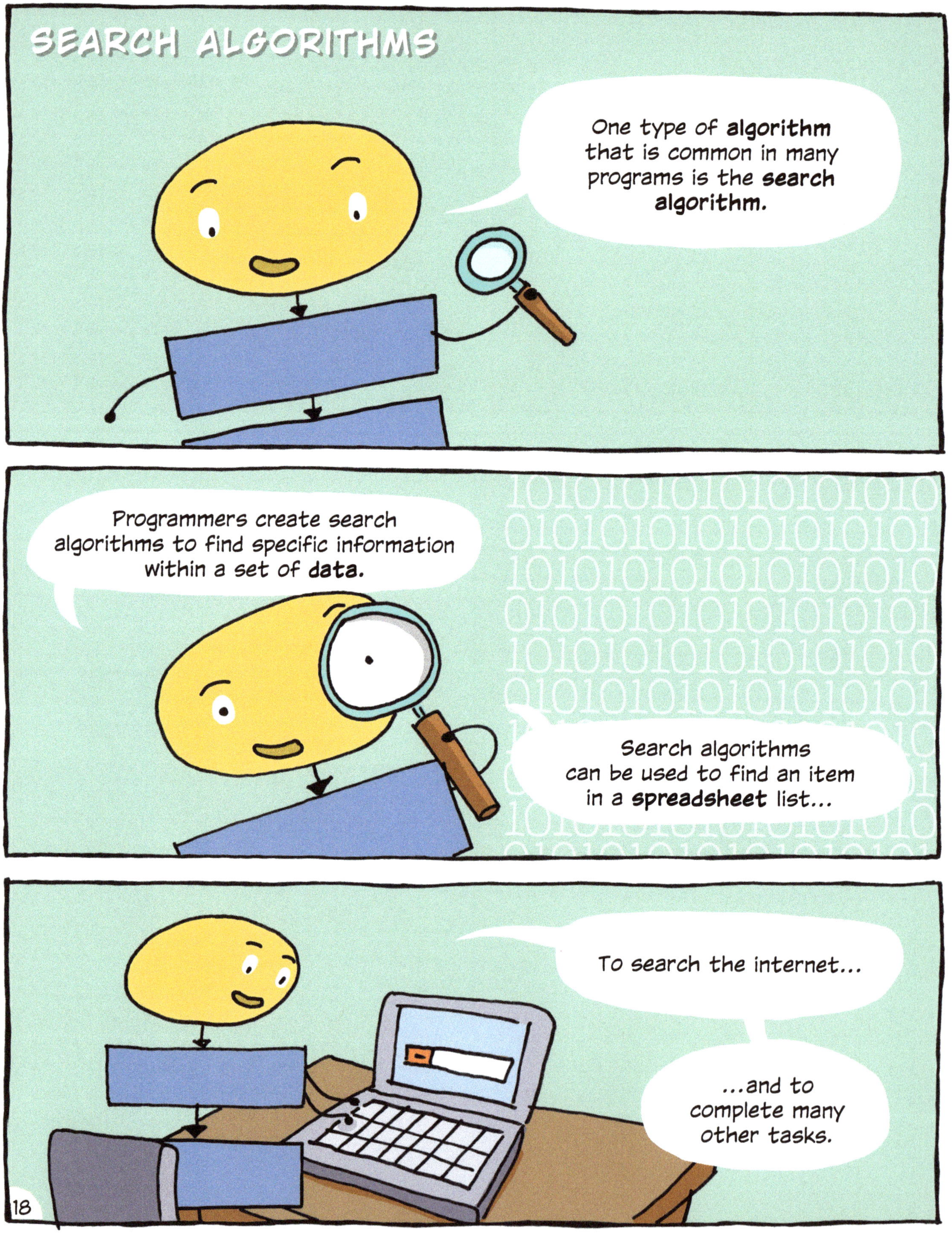

SEARCH ALGORITHMS

One type of **algorithm** that is common in many programs is the **search algorithm.**

Programmers create search algorithms to find specific information within a set of **data.**

Search algorithms can be used to find an item in a **spreadsheet** list...

There are many different search algorithms.
They fit into two types: **sequential searches** and **interval searches.**
start
start
start
start
start
With a sequential search algorithm, the computer checks each item on the list one at a time to find the correct item.
If the first item is not correct,
the computer goes to the next item.
So, we can ask Tasky to find the grapes on this shelf by checking each item one by one...
Until he finds the grapes!

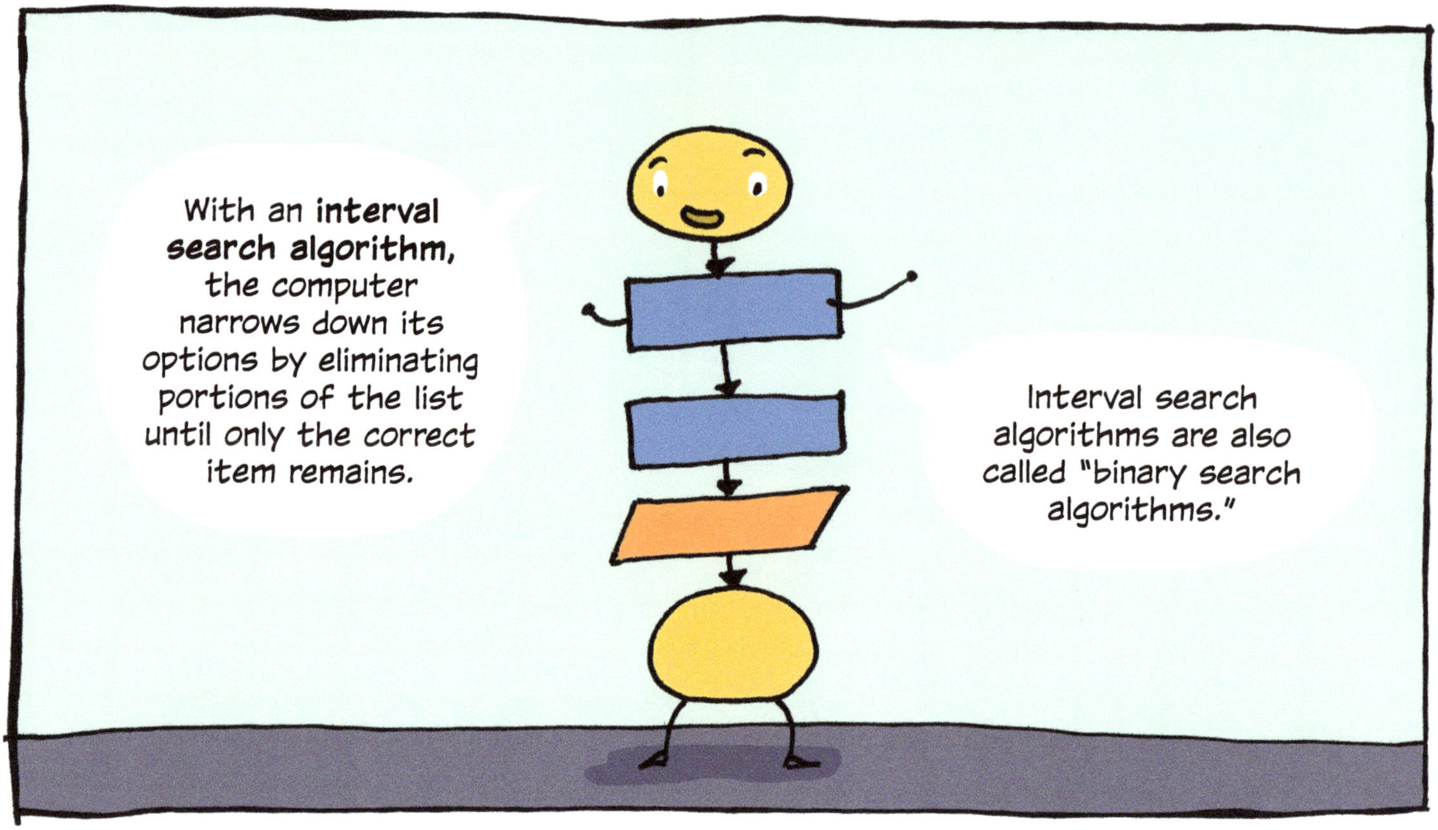

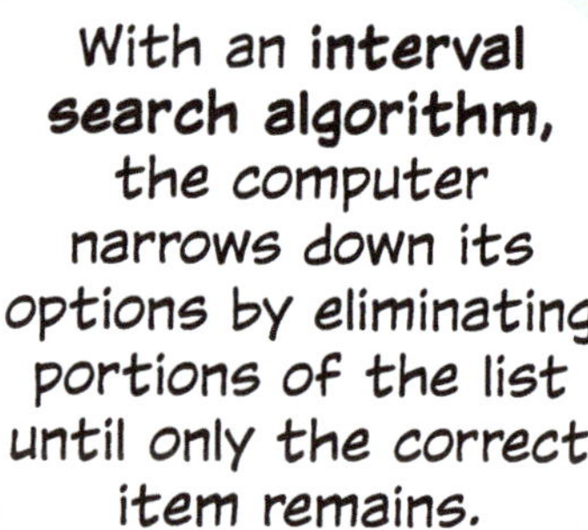

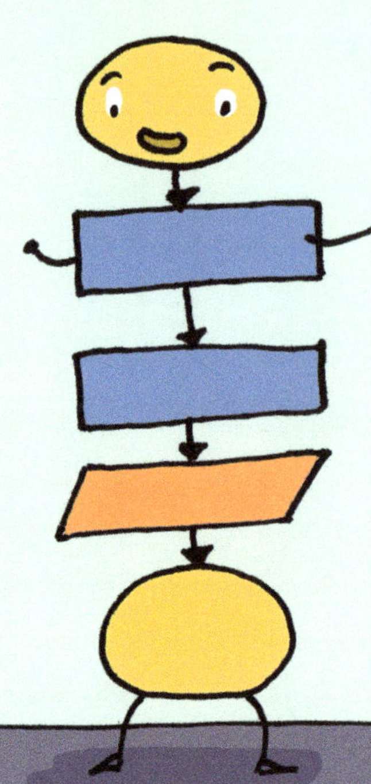

Interval search algorithms are also called "binary search algorithms."

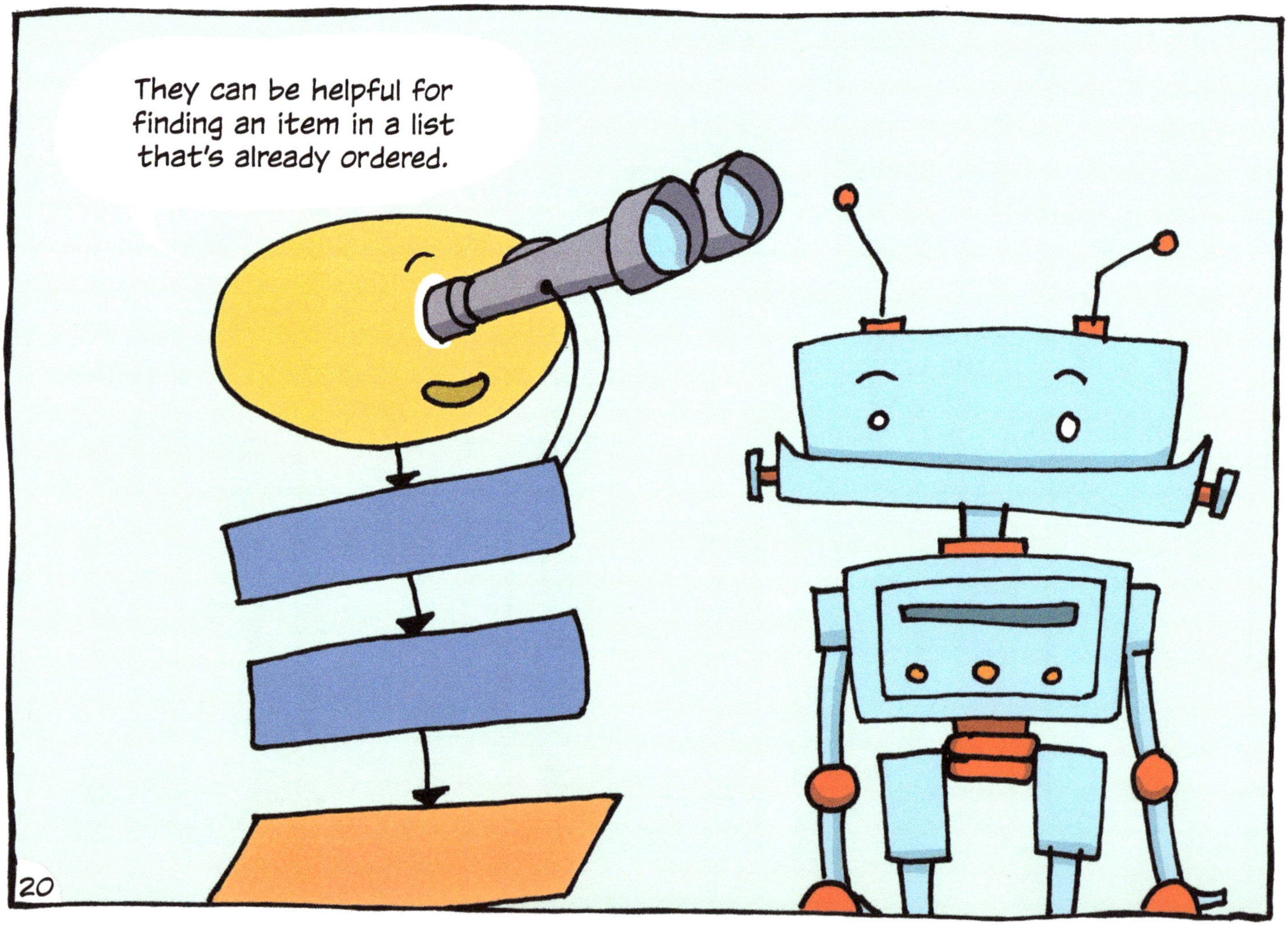

They can be helpful for finding an item in a list that's already ordered.

Each of these boxes contains a fruit. The fruits are arranged in alphabetical order. This time, we want Tasky to find the cherries.

A B C G P S W

The first box Tasky will check is the MIDDLE box.

Grapes

No cherries in there! But, since "cherries" starts with the letter C, Tasky knows they must be to the left, not to the right.

Banana

That means there are only 3 boxes left that could contain the cherries. Again, Tasky will check the middle box.

No cherries yet! But since C comes AFTER B, Tasky knows the cherries cannot be to the left of the banana. So, the cherries must be to the right!

cherries

SORTING ALGORITHMS

For example, I have 16 books that I want to read.

I want to read them in order of length, from the shortest book to the longest.

How can I sort the books so that they're in the correct order?

There are many different kinds of **sorting algorithms** that can be used for different situations...

Let's try using a **bubble sort algorithm** to organize the books.

BUBBLE SORT ALGORITHM
Initial
5 3 8 4 6
Initial unsorted list
Step 1.
5 3 8 4 6
Compare 1st and 2nd (Swap)
Step 2.
3 5 8 4 6
Compare 2nd and 3rd (Do not Swap)
Step 3.
3 5 8 4 6
Compare 3rd and 4th (Swap)
Step 4.
3 5 4 8 6
Compare 4th and 5th (Swap)
Step 5.
3 5 4 6 8
Repeat Step 1-5 until no moreswaps required
In a bubble sort, the elements in a list are sorted in pairs.
The elements in each pair are compared and put in the correct order, one pair at a time.
If two elements are in the wrong order, they get swapped to the correct order.
A bubble sort would work for sorting my books, but it is not the most efficient way to get the job done.

I think I'll try using an **insertion-sort algorithm** to sort the books more quickly.

9 7 6 15 17 5 10 11

9 7 6 15 17 5 10 11

7 9 6 15 17 5 10 11

6 7 9 15 17 5 10 11

6 7 9 15 17 5 10 11

6 7 9 15 17 5 10 11

5 6 7 9 15 17 10 11

5 6 7 9 10 15 17 11

5 6 7 9 10 11 15 17

In an insertion sort, each item is checked one by one, and placed in the correct position.

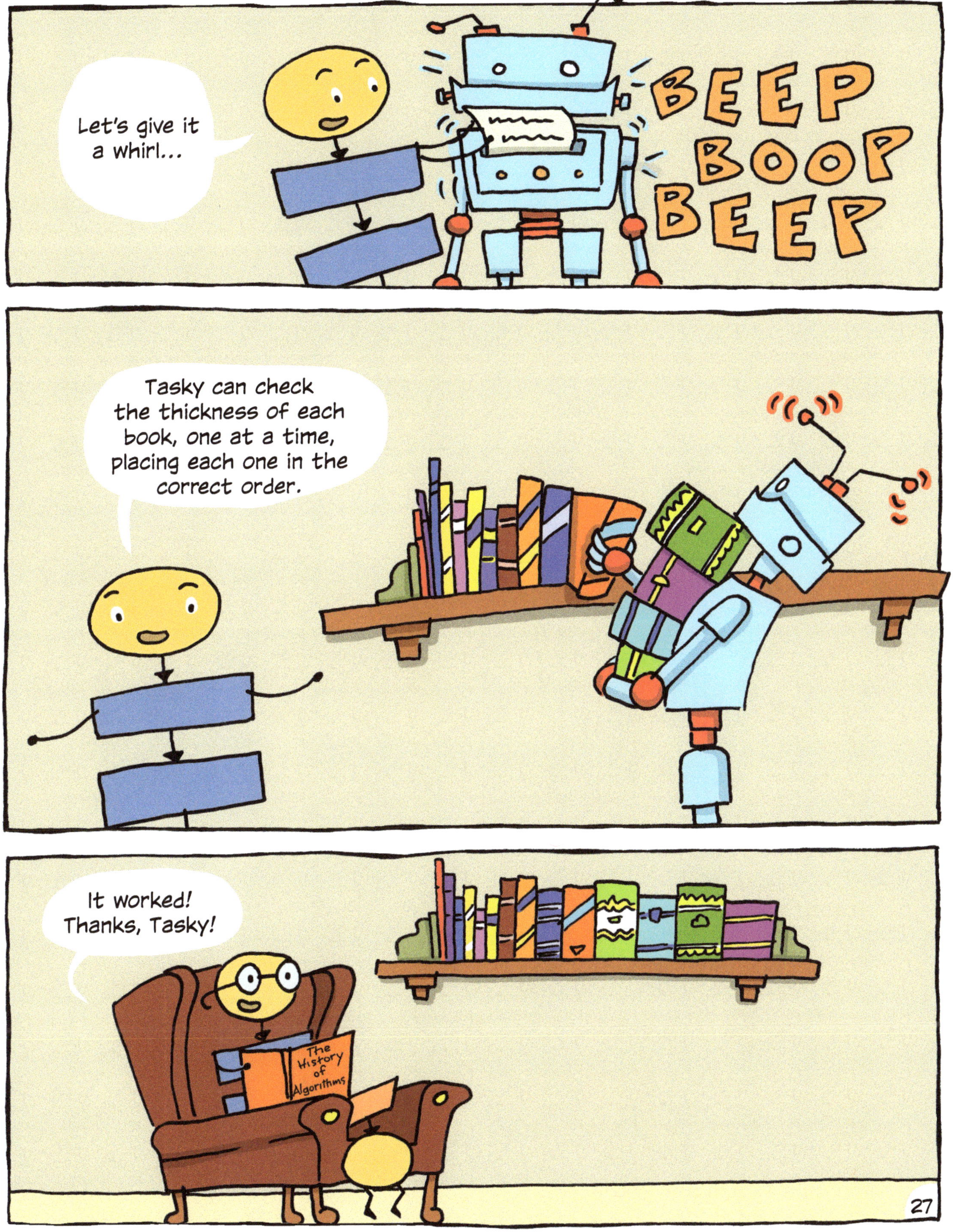

Tasky can check the thickness of each book, one at a time, placing each one in the correct order.

ALGORITHMS IN HISTORY

In the 1800's, an English noblewoman named Ada Lovelace wrote an algorithm for programming a computing machine.
Analytical Engine

The algorithm calculated a list of numbers called Bernoulli numbers, which are useful for computing complicated math problems.
Lovelace's algorithm was one of the very first computer programs ever written.
Today, algorithms are used to help people in so many ways!

I'm an algorithm! How do you think I can help the world?

GLOSSARY

algorithm a set of step-by-step instructions used to write computer programs. Algorithms are also used to solve math problems and other problems.

bubble-sort algorithm a sorting algorithm that tells the computer to put a list of data in the correct order by arranging the data in pairs.

code instructions written in a programming language.

data information that a computer processes or stores.

flow chart a diagram that uses shapes and arrows to show the order of steps that make up a process.

insertion-sort algorithm a sorting algorithm that tells the computer to check each item in a list of data one at a time to put the list in a particular order.

interval search a search algorithm that tells the computer to eliminate chunks of data from a list to find a particular piece of data.

programming language a set of symbols and rules that programmers use to write computer programs.

pseudocode a description of a computer program written in human language.

search algorithm an algorithm that is used to find specific information in a list of data.

sequential search a search algorithm that tells the computer to check each item in a list of data one at a time to find a particular piece of data.

sorting algorithm an algorithm that is used to put a list of data in a particular order.

spreadsheet a document in which data is arranged in a grid.

GO ONLINE

Ready to try making and following algorithms yourself? Go to this website and click on the Algorithm Origami activity to make an origami penguin! You'll find all kinds of fun computer science activities! Click on the Robot Friend activity to find an algorithm game you can play with a pal.

www.worldbook.com/BuildingBlocks

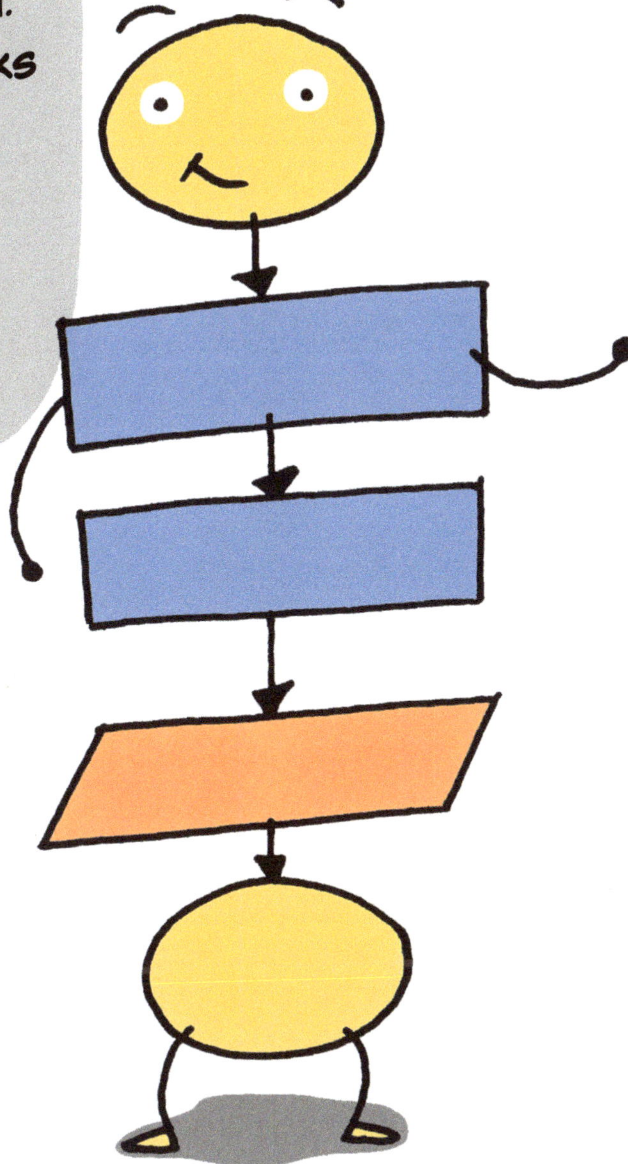

INDEX

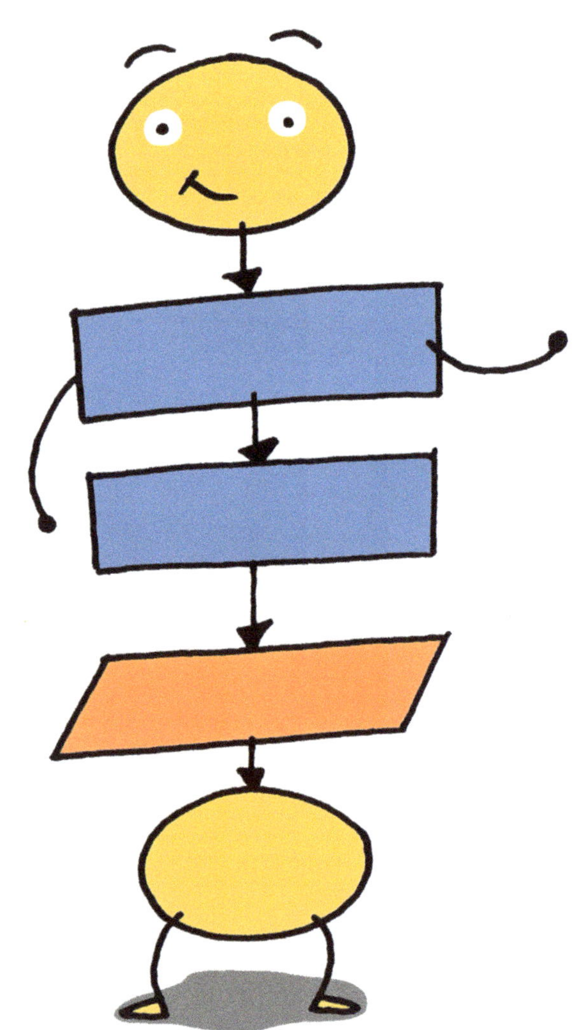

www.ingramcontent.com/pod-product-compliance
Ingram Content Group UK Ltd.
Pitfield, Milton Keynes, MK11 3LW, UK
UKHW061958290726
14090UKWH00021B/1264

9 780716 633822